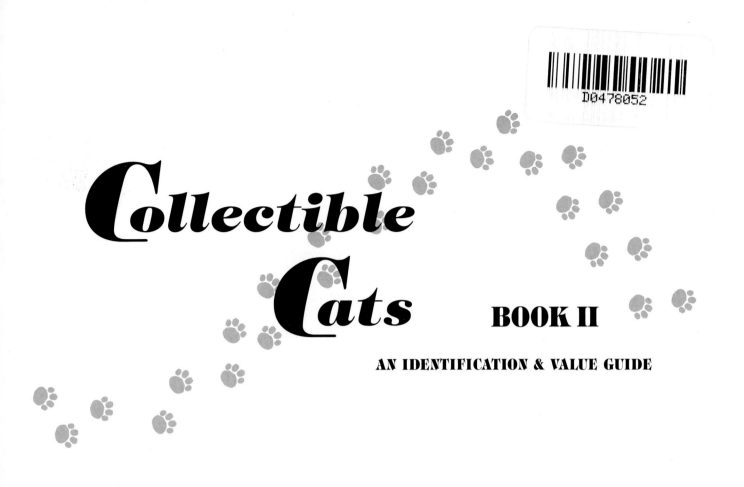

Collectible Cats

BOOK II

AN IDENTIFICATION & VALUE GUIDE

Marbena "Jean" Fyke

Photos by Bob Fyke

COLLECTOR BOOKS

A Division of Schroeder Publishing Co., Inc.

The current values in this book should be used only as a guide. They are not intended to set prices, which vary from one section of the country to another. Auction prices as well as dealer prices vary greatly and are affected by condition as well as demand. Neither the Author nor the Publisher assumes responsibility for any losses that might be incurred as a result of consulting this guide.

On the cover: *Upper right:* Made by Summit Art Glass, Ohio, from Westmoreland molds, 5" long x 4" tall, Westmoreland mark, 1970s. $20.00. *Middle left:* Bank, head locks to body with a brass lock, 1940s, 8" tall. $40.00. *Middle center:* Tin-lithograph sign, new reproduction of old sign, still available, 12" tall x 8¾" wide. $10.00. *Middle right:* "Cheshire Cat," Disney Collection, 5" tall. This was only available to members. $135.00. *Bottom left:* Postcard, $4.00. *Bottom center:* Solid "Verdigris" brass cat, 10¾" tall, 1992. Verdigris is an aging process which gives the piece a look of being old. $90.00 – 95.00. *Bottom right:* Door stop, new, plaster, 10½" tall x 8" wide. $15.00.

Book design by: Karen Long
Cover design by: Karen Geary

SEARCHING FOR A PUBLISHER?

We are always looking for knowledgable people considered to be experts within their fields. If you feel that there is a real need for a book on your collectible subject and have a large comprehensive collection, contact Collector Books.

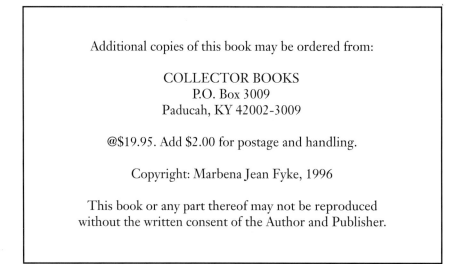
Printed by IMAGE GRAPHICS, INC., Paducah, Kentucky

Dedication

This book is dedicated to Rachel, Bobby, and Christopher who brighten every day of my life.

In Memory

In memory of Tom my faithful feline companion for 18 years.

Acknowledgments

Many, many thanks to the following people who allowed me to photograph pieces from their collections: Gary Beegle, Judy Carroll, Therese Cavalari, Mary Clayton, Chris Countryman, Richard Ehlenberg, Lorraine Greenwood, Marilyn Havlicek, Peg McDermott, Dona Pisano, Amanda Sewall, Robin Tweedie, and Harriet and Howie Zuckerman.

Special Thanks

Special thanks to Tennessee who is always there for me, and lets me upset his house to do our photo shoots.

Contents

Introduction

When I did the first book I had no idea that there would be a second one, but here it is.

In the past two years I have met and corresponded with fellow cat collectors from all over the country. There are a lot of us "cataholics" out there. Cats remain the number one pet and therefore a plethora of cat items can be found to add to one's collection.

When we started photographing for this book I had no trouble finding people that would allow me to photograph portions of their collections. I was also amazed at how many cats I have added to my own collection.

In this book I have included Steiff's, paper items, postcards, handcrafted items, tapestries, as well as, black cat, Garfield, and glass.

Chalkware, resin, bisque, and lusterware are terms used to described many of the pieces. The following are brief descriptions of those terms:

Chalkware is made of gypsum or plaster of Paris. The earliest chalkware figures were made from 1860 to 1890. The later and most commonly known pieces were made as carnival prizes for shooting galleries, guessing your weight and age, and pitch ball games.

Lusterware was made by applying a metallic glaze to once fired pieces. These pieces were fired again resulting in a wonderful iridescent finish. The pieces seen most often are the tea sets made in Japan during the 1930s and 1940s.

Bisque is earthenware that has been fired only once and then decorated. It does not have the shiny surface of pieces that have been glazed and fired a second time.

Resin is a mixture of plastic and porcelain that is poured cold into molds and then heated to harden. Resin pieces have remarkable lifelike detail.

As in the first book I have included old, new, and in between. The quality of some of the things being produced in China and Taiwan is really amazing. Figures made by Enesco, Sandy Cast, and others are also very finely detailed. Some of Enesco's resin figures look like they will sit up and meow at you.

I believe, as do many of my fellow collectors, that if a piece pleases you, buy it, whether old or new. Of course if you are strictly a purest you will only buy older items. Whatever your pleasure, may you enjoy collecting as much as I do.

I hope you enjoy this book as much as I have enjoyed compiling it.

Here's to Cats! Cats! and more Cats!

Black Cat, Shafford, and Others

Shafford decanter, 8" tall. $45.00

Shafford egg cup, 3" tall. $35.00 – 40.00.

Single figurine, 3¾". Maker unknown. $10.00.

Shafford figurine, 2¾" tall. $15.00.

Shafford salt and pepper shakers, 4" tall. $25.00.

Set of Wales cats. Mama, 2½"; babies, 1¼". $15.00 – $20.00 set.

Wales salt and pepper shakers, 3" tall. $15.00.

Ashtray, 5" tall, 4½" wide. Has dark green eyes, could be Shafford but I'm not positive. $30.00.

Salt and pepper shakers with rhinestone eyes, 5" long. $15.00.

Bookend, 5½" tall. I seem to be destined to find single bookends. This could be Shafford, I'm not sure. $15.00.

Salt and pepper shakers. $15.00.

Bookend, 5½" tall. $15.00.

Letter Holder. I believe that the hole between his paws is for a coil of stamps. $20.00.

Chalkware marked Manor Ware, 1940, 3¼" tall. $35.00.

Ceramic cat, 1970s, 16" tall. $20.00.

Salt and pepper shakers, 6" & 5½". $20.00 pair.

Early chalkware bank, 13¼" tall. $125.00 – 150.00.

Stylized ceramic cat, 16¼" tall, dark green painted eyes as with the Shafford cats, no mark, 1950s. $35.00 – 40.00.

Pair of ceramic cats, 11¼" tall, very deco, 1940s. $40.00 pair.

Porcelain, marked Royal Crown Germany, 1940s, 10" long, 5" tall. $65.00.

Books

Babette published by Harper Bros., 1937. $30.00.

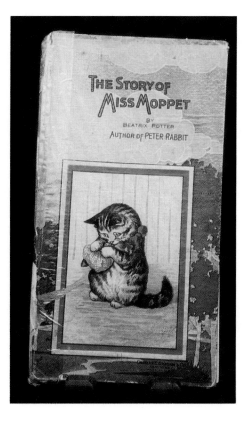

Left: *The Story of Miss Moppet* by Beatrix Potter, published by Charles E. Graham Co., NY. $20.00.

Friends of the Family published by The American News Co., 1880. Fine engravings. Cover bad, book in excellent condition. $45.00 as is.

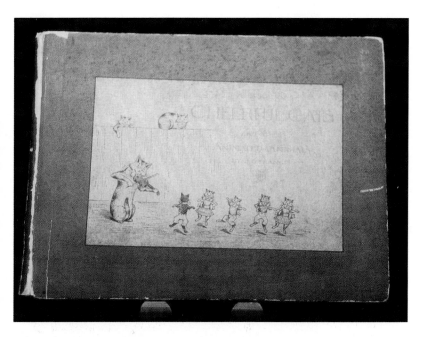

Cheerful Cats published by The Century Co., 1903. I wish you could see the wonderful steel engravings in this book. $55.00.

Scat Cat by Sally Francis, published by Platt & Munk, 1940. $20.00.

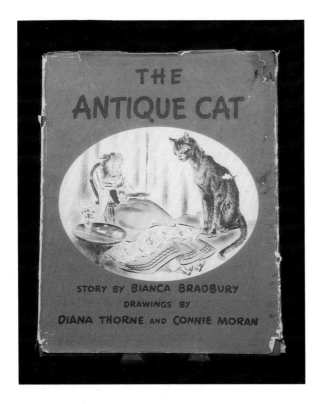

Fluffy Puffy and Muffy published by Samuel Lowe & Co., 1944. $10.00 as is.

The Antique Cat published by John Winston Co., 1945. $25.00.

The Literary Cat published by Running Press, Philadelphia, PA, 1990, 3¼" x 2¾". $10.00.

Moses the Kitten published by St. Martins Press, 1984. $15.00.

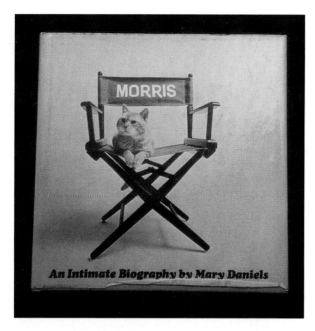

Morris by Marg Daniels, published by William Morrow Co., New York, NY, 1974. $20.00.

Cats! Cats! Cats! published by Hallmark, 1973. $10.00.

Catundra published by Crolier Enterprises Inc., 1978. Very fine illustrations. $20.00.

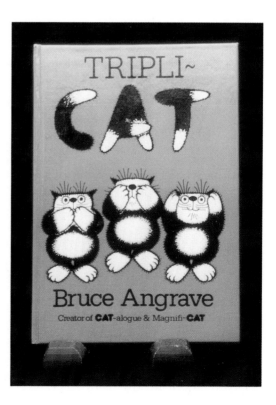

Tripli published by Collins & Sons, Glascow and London, 1978. $15.00.

Cat's Companion published by Pellham Books, 1986. $10.00.

Catmopolitan published by Pocket Books, 1987. This is a takeoff on *Cosmopolitan* magazine. It's one of my favorite cat collectibles. $25.00.

Catcalendar Cats published by Workman, New York, NY, 1981. $45.00.

Garfield

Talking Telephone. After each ring he has a smart remark such as "It's the President, Yah" or "I'm not getting it." It says 10 different things. $40.00.

Trivet, 9" x 4¾". $10.00.

Hallmark 1992 Christmas ornament, 2½". $10.00.

Everyone needs a Garfield yo-yo. $10.00.

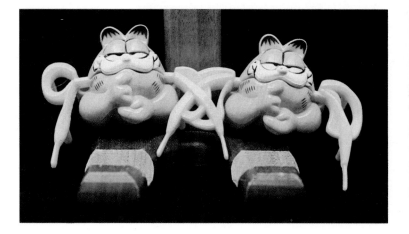

Would you believe shoe lace holders?! $5.00.

The pesky one himself in a foil picture. $10.00.

Danbury Mint Plate, "I deny everything." $25.00.

Danbury Mint Plate, "Simple minds, Simple pleasures." $25.00.

Danbury Mint Plate, "Dreams can take you anywhere." $25.00.

Danbury Mint Plate, "Cats have fun too." $25.00.

Danbury Mint, "I'll rise but I won't shine." $25.00.

Danbury Mint, "Today I composed myself." $25.00.

Danbury Mint, "Today all nine of my lives flashed before me." $25.00.

Danbury Mint, "Sleep the perfect exercise." $25.00.

Danbury Mint, "Friends are forever." $25.00.

Danbury Mint, "And now for desert." $25.00.

Danbury Mint, "It's not the having, it's the getting." $25.00.

Danbury Mint, "My horoscope told me to start an art project today." $25.00.

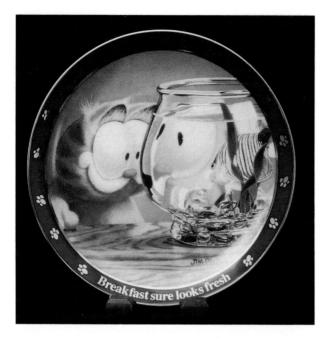

Danbury Mint, "Breakfast sure looks fresh." $25.00.

Danbury Mint, "Today I looked at a new condo." $25.00.

The following 6 photos are of a set currently being issued by the Danbury Mint. $35.00 each.

"On Vacation," 5½".

"King of the Jungle," 4" tall.

"Cat Nap," 4" long x 2½" wide.

"Sitting Pretty," 4" tall.

"The Gourmet," 4¼" long x 2½" tall.

"Mid-night Serenade," 5½" tall.

The following 9 photos are from a series of books published by the United Features Publications, 1981 – 1984. $10.00 each.

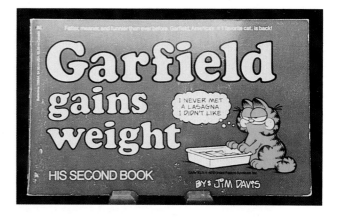

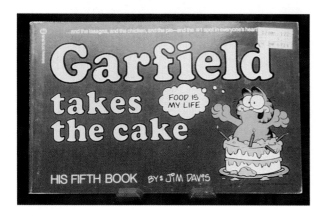

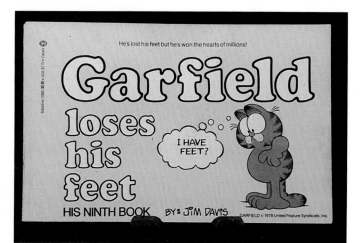

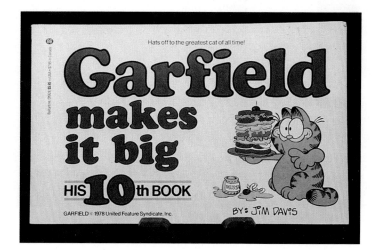

McDonald's coffee mugs given away in the western states. $8.00.

McDonald's coffee mugs given away in the western states. $8.00.

Juice glass, 4" tall. Not sure who put this out. $5.00.

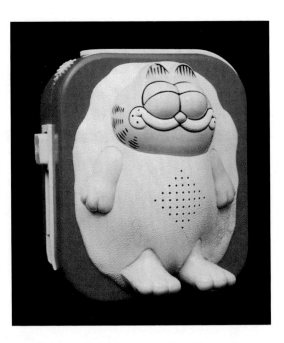

McDonald's coffee mugs given away in the western states. $8.00.

Cassette tape player, runs on batteries, 8" x 8". $15.00.

Clock, 9" tall. $25.00.

Nighty-Night Garfield, 9" tall. $25.00.

This one says it all, 9" tall. $25.00.

Souvenir of Colorado, 9½" tall. $25.00.

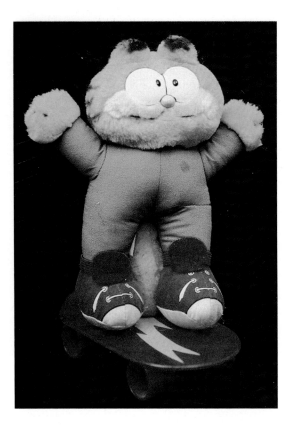

On a skateboard, 9½" tall. $25.00.

Garfield in a globe 2¾" tall. Press the white button in front and he blows bubbles. $10.00.

Pin dish, 4" tall. $10.00.

Vase, 5½" tall. $5.00.

Glass

Paperweight, 3¾". $20.00.

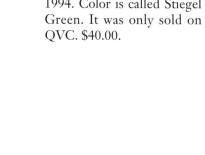

Nightlight, marked Antonette, new, 6¼" tall. $15.00.

Fenton alley cat, 11" tall, 1994. Color is called Stiegel Green. It was only sold on QVC. $40.00.

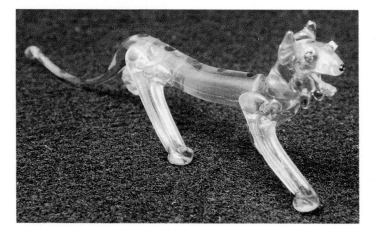

Powder jar, French, marked Derteux, France, 1930s. $65.00 – 75.00.

Handblown, 4" long x 1½" tall, 1950s. $20.00.

Handblown, 1" tall. $20.00 pair.

Handblown, 2" long x 2¾" tall. $15.00.

Wine pitcher, 8" tall, marked WMF Germany, not sure of the age. $30.00.

Three Kittens plate, 1900 souvenir from Asbury Park. $35.00 – 40.00.

Waterford, 6" long x 4½" tall. Still available from Cashes of Ireland. $180.00.

Tiffin Glass, 4¾" tall. $45.00.

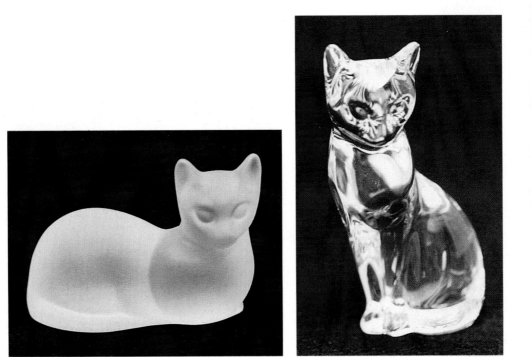

Lenox. These cats are called "Prim & Proper." Frosted one, 3½" long x 3" tall; clear one, 4¼" tall. $125.00 pair.

Bell, 1989, 8" tall. $20.00.

I believe the following four photos may have been made by Boyd Glass or possibly Mosser Glass. They are 2¾" tall. $15.00 – 20.00 each.

A. $20.00. B. $25.00.

33

Artist signed Fenton. $15.00 each.

A. $15.00. B. $20.00.

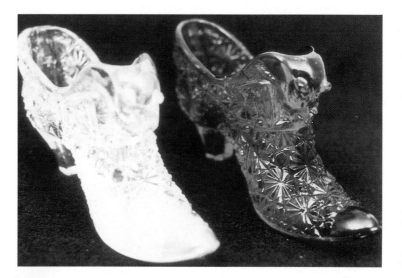

A. $15.00. B. $15.00 – 20.00.

A. $25.00. B. $20.00.

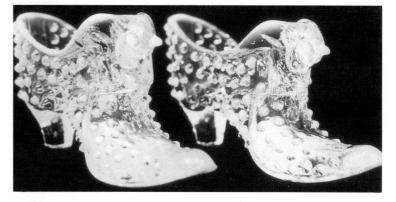

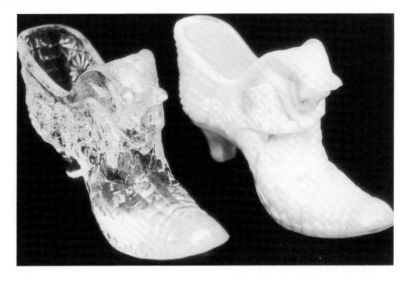

A. $15.00 – 20.00. B. $25.00.

A. $10.00. B. $15.00 – 20.00.

A. $15.00. B. $15.00.

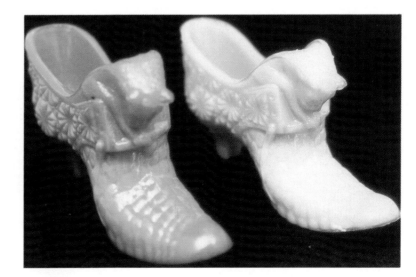

A. $10.00 – 15.00. B. $10.00 – 15.00.

A. $10.00.

A. $15.00. B. $20.00 – 25.00.

A. $20.00. B. $15.00 – 20.00.

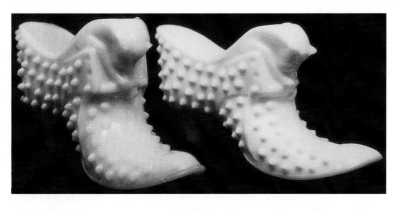

A. $25.00. B. $15.00.

A. Degenhart, signed. $35.00 – 45.00.

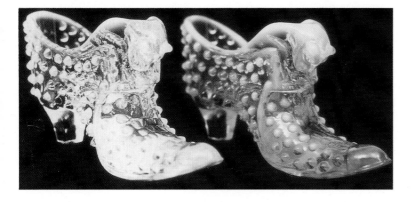

A. $15.00 – 20.00. B. $20.00.

New sun catcher. $8.00 – 10.00.

9 Lives giveaway tumblers. $10.00 each.

Snow globe, 1985, 4½" tall. $25.00.

The following eight items were made by Summit Art Glass, Ohio, from Westmoreland molds, 5" long x 4" tall, Westmoreland mark, 1970s.

$20.00.

$35.00.

$30.00.

$45.00.

$45.00.

$35.00.

$40.00.

$45.00.

Murano made in Italy, 7¼" tall. $60.00.

Glass egg with reverse painting. This is an ancient Chinese art form. Egg is blown, leaving a small hole through which the artist paints. 3½" tall and sits on a birchwood stand. $65.00.

Crystal ball made by the Franklin Mint, solid brass holder. $250.00.

Covered candy dish, new, 7" tall. $25.00.

The following three items were salt dishes made by Boyd Glass, 1½" tall. $20.00 each.

Fenton, artist signed, 3½" tall. $20.00.

The following three items were made by Fenton between 1977 and 1993, 3¾" tall. $20.00 each.

Fenton March birthday cat, 3¾" tall. $25.00.

Fenton, 1989, 3¾" tall. $25.00.

The next three items are by Fenton, artist signed, 1993, 3¾" long. $20.00. each.

Made by Boyd Glass, hard to find color, 3½" tall, 1970s. $35.00 – 40.00.

Baby bottle, 1940s, 7" tall. $30.00.

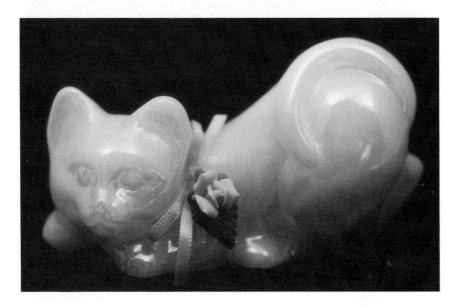

Fenton, 1994, 3¾" long. $25.00.

Boyd Glass, 4" long. $25.00.

Blown glass, 4¼" tall, new. $25.00.

The following three photos were furnished by Gary Beegle of Montgomery, New York. He has one of the largest collections of cartoon glasses.

"Figaro" tumbler part of a set of 12 issued in 1940. There were four sizes available. $20.00.

"Aristocats" tumbler, made in France, new, writing on tumbler "Les Aristochats." $10.00.

"Rufus" tumbler, issued in 1977 by Brockway Pepsi. $15.00.

Handcrafted Items and Tapestries

Doorstop made from detergent bottle, all hand sewn, 16" tall. $25.00.

Ceramic doll, 15" tall. $25.00.

Crewel picture, 8" x 10", Tom Kitten. $40.00.

Hand-sewn stuffed doll, 21" tall. $35.00.

Ceramic doll, 22" tall, artist signed. $30.00.

Hand-decorated stuffed kitty, 14½" tall. The entire bridal ensemble is hand stitched. Kitty even has a money bag. $75.00.

Handmade, 8" tall. $15.00.

Hand-decorated stuffed kitty, cloths are hand sewn, 9" tall. $20.00.

Crocheted cat, 1½" long. $10.00.

Patchwork cat, 7" tall. $20.00.

Handmade, 17" long. $20.00.

Handmade child's mittens, 1930s. $20.00.

Crewel picture, 16" x 16". $65.00.

Chessie handkerchief made for the Chesapeake & Ohio Railway, 8" x 8". $15.00.

Crochet plaques, 3" wide, new. $10.00 pair.

Crocheted sofa doily, 25" x 15", 1930. $25.00.

Tapestry, 1940s, 41" x 20".
$25.00.

Tapestry, 1920s, 41" x 20".
$65.00.

Tapestry, 1920s, 41" x 20".
$45.00.

Tapestry, 1930s, 41" x 20". $45.00.

Crewel pillow cover, 23" x 18½". $55.00.

Embroidered picture, 1920s, 15½" x 16½". $45.00.

Framed tapestry from the 1920s, 20" x 18¼". $65.00 – 70.00.

Kitchenware

Cookie jar, Shawnee Puss & Boots, 10" tall. $135.00.

Cookie jar, new, 12" long x 9" tall. $25.00.

Cookie jar, 1950s, 7½" long x 6" tall. $45.00.

Left: Cookie jar, McCoy, 1940s, 13" tall. Paint is bad. $25.00 as is.

Cookie jar, new, 11" long x 8" tall. $25.00.

Cookie jar, new, 8" tall. $20.00.

Cookie jar, new, 13" tall. $25.00.

Teapot, 1993, sold on QVC, 8½" tall. $25.00.

Teapot, 1992, 9½" tall. $20.00.

Teapot, new, 13" long x 6" tall. $20.00.

Teapot, Avon, 1993, 9" tall. $35.00.

Teapot, new, 7" tall. $15.00.

Teapot, new, 8" long x 5½" tall. $15.00.

Teapot, new, 4" tall. $5.00.

Teapot, new, 5½" tall. $10.00.

Teapot, new, 5" tall. $5.00.

Teapot, 1987, 9½" tall. $20.00.

Child's drinking cup, new. $5.00.

Mayonaise pot, 1950s, 4" tall. $25.00.

Bathroom brush holder, 9" tall, new. $15.00.

Just a cute coffee mug, one of 45 in my collection. $5.00.

One glass of a set of 8, 4" tall. $25.00 set.

Pair of porcelain napkin rings, 1940s, 3¼" tall. I have 4 of each style. $10.00 each.

Creamer and sugar to the teapot in the bottom left photo on page 55, 4¾" tall. $15.00 pair.

Spoon rest, new, 8½" tall. $5.00 – 7.00.

String holder, 1930s, 8" tall x 4" wide, chalkware. $45.00 – 50.00.

Water kettle, new, enameled 3¾" x 7½". $20.00.

Czechoslovakian lusterware creamer, 1930s, 7½" tall. $45.00.

Porcelain creamer, 1930s, 6¾" tall. $25.00.

Porcelain string holder, 1940s, signed Adele Reynolds, 5" tall. $30.00 – 40.00.

Porcelain milk pitcher, impressed numbers on bottom, very deco looking, 1920s, 8" tall. $65.00.

Shawnee creamer, 1940s, 5" tall. $45.00.

String holder, 1950s, marked Japan, 6½". $25.00.

Porcelain trivet, 1940s, 8½" long x 3¾" wide. $55.00 – 65.00.

Salt and pepper shakers. $8.00 pair.

Pair of hanging salt and pepper shakers. $10.00 pair.

Avon salt and pepper shakers. $15.00 pair.

Salt and pepper shakers, 1950s. $10.00 pair.

Hanging salt and pepper shakers, 1940s.
$30.00 pair.

Salt and pepper shakers, meow when they are shaken. $20.00 pair.

Salt and pepper shakers, 1950s, Lefton China. $20.00 pair.

Salt and pepper shakers. $10.00 pair.

Salt and pepper shakers. $10.00 – 12.00 pair.

Salt and pepper shakers. $10.00 pair.

Salt and pepper shakers.
$10.00 – 12.00 pair.

Salt and pepper shakers.
$10.00 – 12.00 pair.

Metal and Wood

Pair of brass cats, 1970s. Large, 6" tall; small, 4" tall. $20.00 pr.

Bronze, no marks, new, 6" long. $75.00.

Solid verdigris brass cat, 10¾" tall, 1992. Verdigris is an aging process which gives the piece a look of being old. $90.00 – 95.00.

Brass bank made for the Union National Bank, 1986. $35.00.

Silver-plated bronze pin tray, 1920s, 6" wide. $65.00.

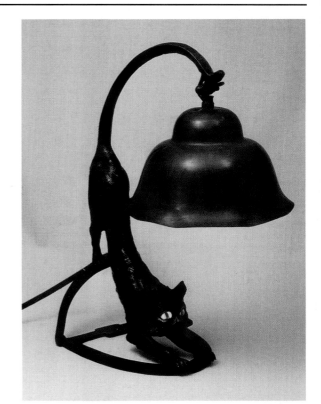

Solid brass lamp, 17" tall, eyes light up. In plate 184 in the first book I pictured the cast-iron reproduction of this lamp. $375.00 – 395.00.

Reproduction cast-iron bank, 4½" tall. $25.00.

Pewter frame, new, 2½" tall x 2" wide. $10.00 – 15.00.

Ring holder made of zinc alloy silver, has rhinestone eyes, 3¾" tall. $10.00.

Brass trivet, 8" tall. 1955. $25.00.

Brass corkscrew, marked Israel, 1970, 3¼" wide x 3" tall. $20.00.

Enameled cigarette case, 1950s, 3¾" x 2½". $40.00.

Brass, 5" tall x 7" long, 1970. $25.00.

Cast metal pincushion, 4" long x 2½" tall, 1910. $45.00. Note the cat stickpin. $35.00 – 40.00.

Austrian bronze, 1920s, 2" long. $185.00 – 200.00.

Bronze, marked Germany, 1920s, 3" tall. $100.00.

Silver-plated bank, 1960s, 5½" tall. $20.00.

Brass, 12½" tall, 1970s. $15.00 – 20.00.

Cast-iron doorstop, 1930s, 7¾" tall. $85.00 – 95.00.

Solid brass, 1985, 3¼" tall x 4" long. $25.00.

Left: Cast-iron doorstop, 10¾" tall, 1930s. $45.00 – 50.00.

Right: Cast-iron doorstop, new, 12¾" tall. $25.00.

Left: Cast-iron doorstop, 9½" tall, not sure of age, appears to be old. $50.00 – 55.00.

Right: Cast-iron doorstop, new glass eyes, 11½" tall. $25.00.

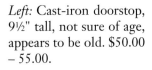

Cast-iron doorstop, 1940s, 10" long x 5" tall. $55.00.

Cast-iron doorstop, 1970s, 7¾" tall. $35.00 – 45.00.

Pewter, 1¾" tall, new. $20.00.

Whimsical wooden cat, new, 12¼" long, hand painted. $35.00.

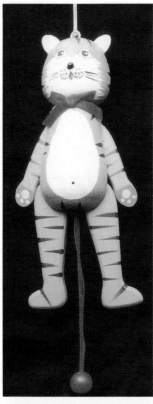

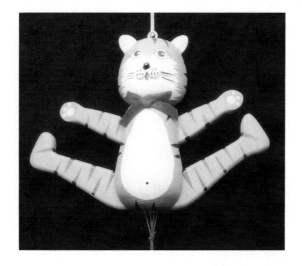

Left and top: Handmade wooden puppet, 1975, 7" tall. $25.00.

Right: Danish wooden cat, 1950s, 9½" tall. $25.00.

Right: Polish wooden cat filled with 8 little cats. Large one, 6¼" tall; little ones, 2" tall, new. $25.00.

Monkey pod, wood, made for QVC, 1991, 14½" tall. $45.00.

3-D wooden cat, tail moves to hang down, new, 14" tall. $25.00.

Wooden, made in Portugal, 11¾" long, new. $15.00 – 20.00.

Mexican, hand painted, 3¼" tall. $10.00.

Mexican, painted wood, 7" long x 3" tall. $15.00 – 20.00.

Mexican, hand painted. 4¾" tall. 10.00.

Droste chocolate box, 1920, 7" x 4½". $35.00.

The following six photos are folk art hand-painted birchwood boxes, 2½" wide, new. $10.00 each.

Tin-lithograph sign, new reproduction of old sign, still available, 12" tall x 8¾" wide. $10.00.

New tin, 8" tall. $10.00.

Candy tin, new, 4½" x 3". $10.00.

Candy tin, 1940s, 6" x 4½". $35.00.

Taffy tin, made in England, 1980, 3¾". $15.00.

Taffy tin, made in England, 5" wide, new. $10.00.

New tin, 7" wide. $10.00.

Cookie tin, new, 7" wide. $15.00.

Handmade wooden wall hanger, 11¾" tall. When cats are fed you turn heart one way ("fed"), not fed you turn it the other ("hungry"). $25.00.

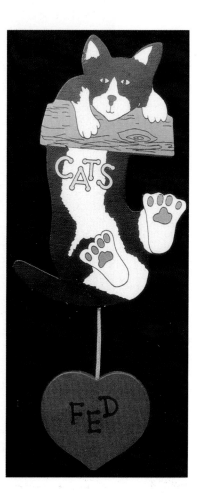

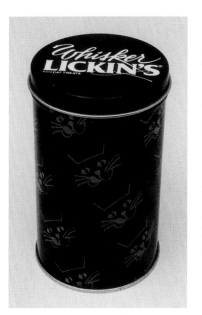

Whisker Lickin's cat food tin, new, 4¼" tall. $8.00 – 10.00.

Cookie tin, new, 7" wide. $10.00.

Miniatures and Smalls

Ceramic, 1950s, 3" tall. $5.00 – 10.00.

Brass, marked Germany, 1"
tall. $25.00 – 35.00.

German porcelain. Mama, 3" tall x 4" long; baby, 1". $35.00 set.

Goebel, part of a set, 1". $15.00.

Goebel. Mama, 3" long x 2" tall; baby, 1½" tall. $30.00 – 40.00 pair.

Goebel, part of a set, 1" x 2½". $15.00.

Bone china set. Mama, 3"; kittens, 1". $15.00 set.

German porcelain, 1930s, 2¼" wide x 1½" tall. Very unusual piece as monkeys are usually depicted doing the three no evils. $40.00.

German porcelain, marked Metzger, 1940s, 5" wide x 2" tall. $45.00.

German porcelain, marked Metzger, 1940s, 2¾" tall. $35.00 – 40.00.

Arts & crafts molded clay cat, 1965, 3¼" tall. $15.00.

Stone bisque, 1940s, no mark, 2¼" tall. $20.00.

Porcelain, 1950s, 1" tall x 1" wide. $10.00.

Ceramic toothpick holder, 1940s, 1¾" tall. $25.00.

Bisque, made in China, new, 2½" tall. $5.00 each.

Molded resin, new, 3¾". $10.00.

Bisque, made in China, new, 2½" tall. $5.00 each.

Bone china, new. Mama, 2½" tall; kittens, 1" tall. $10.00 set.

Stone bisque, 1940s, no mark, 3½" x 3". $20.00.

Porcelain, 1940s, 3" long. $15.00.

Bone china, 2" tall. $10.00 set.

Bone china, 1950s, 2½" tall. $8.00 – 10.00.

Bone china, 2" tall, new. $8.00 – 10.00.

Bone china, 3" tall. $8.00 – 10.00.

Molded resin, new, 2¼" tall, glass eyes. $15.00.

Flocked cat with puffy yarn tail, 1940s, 3" tall. $10.00.

Bone china set. Mama, 2" tall; kittens, 1" tall. $10.00 set.

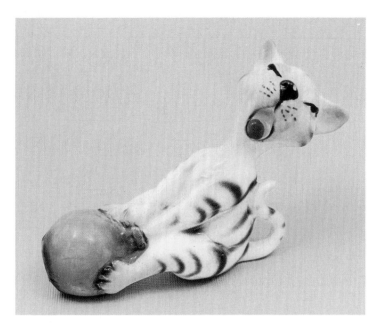

Porcelain, 1940s, 4" long x 3" tall. $15.00.

Bone china, marked England, 3" wide x 1¾" tall. $20.00.

Porcelain, no marks, believe they are German, 1930s. $65.00 set.

Beatrix Potter's "Mittens & Moppet" made by Bestwick in England, 1989, 3¾" tall. $40.00 – 45.00.

Beatrix Potter's "Tom Kitten with Butterfly" made by Bestwick in England, 3½" tall, 1989. $35.00 – 40.00.

Beatrix Potter's "Susan" made by Bestwick in England, 4" tall, 1983. $55.00.

Beatrix Potter's "Ribby and Patty Pan" made by Bestwick in England, 3¼" tall, 1991. $40.00 – 45.00.

Porcelain, 1940s, marked Japan, 3" tall. $15.00.

Porcelain toothpick holder, 1940s, 3" tall. $20.00.

Bisque, marked Germany, 1920s, 3¼" tall. $20.00.

Bisque, new, made in China, 3" tall. $5.00 set.

Ceramic, 1950s, 3" tall. $10.00.

Porcelain thimbles, new, 1" tall. $5.00 each.

Plastic, part of a Disney series, 1950s, 1" tall. $15.00.

Real fur and leather, new, 1½" tall. $10.00. set

Chalkware, 1950s, 3" x 3". $20.00.

Bone china made by Lefton, ½" tall x 1¾" long. $20.00.

Ceramic, 1940s, no marks, could be German. Large, 3" x 2"; small, 1¼" tall. $20.00 set.

Porcelain, 1950s, 3¼" tall x 2½" wide. $15.00 set.

Very early stone cat, 2" long x 1¾" tall. Have yet to find out the exact age. $45.00.

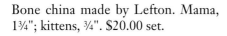

Bone china made by Lefton. Mama, 1¾"; kittens, ¾". $20.00 set.

Bone china, Lefton. Mama, 1¾" x 2½"; kittens, 1". $20.00 set.

Harvey Knox kingdom, new, 2½" long x 2" tall. $20.00.

Porcelain musicians, 1940s, 2" tall, real whiskers. $20.00 pair.

Molded resin, new, 2½" tall. $10.00.

Porcelain musicians, 1940s, made in England, 3½" tall. $25.00 pair.

Chalkware cats, 1¾" tall. I do not know exact age. $15.00 pair.

Ceramic, 1950s, 2¼" long x 2" tall. $10.00.

Ceramic, 1950s. Mama, 4" tall; kittens, 2½" tall. $15.00 set.

Piano baby, German, 3¼" tall, 1920s. $35.00 – 45.00.

A. Bisque, 1920s, 1½" tall. $15.00. B. Porcelain glazed with gold, 1940s, 1½" x 1". $10.00.

Bisque toothpick holder, 3" tall x 2¼" wide, 1930s. $35.00 – 40.00.

A. Stone bisque, marked Japan, 1940s, 2¼" tall. $10.00. B. Same as A, 1½" tall. $5.00.

Porcelain lusterware toothpick holder, 3" tall x 3½" wide. $35.00 – 45.00.

Staffordshire cottage cat, 1910, 2" tall. $65.00 – 70.00.

Goebel, part of a set of 4, ¼" tall. $30.00 – 35.00.

Bone china cats, 1950s, 1½" tall. $7.00 – 10.00 each.

A. Porcelain, 1950s, 1½". $10.00. B. Snow cat (like snow babies), 1940s, porcelain, 1½" tall. $15.00. C. Bone china, 1950s, 1½" tall. $10.00.

Bone china, 1970s. Mama, 2½"; kittens, 1½". $20.00 set.

A. Molded resin, new, 3½". $15.00. B. Country Critter, glass eyes, 3½" tall. $20.00.

Museum reproduction of a Netsuke, 2½" tall. $25.00.

Hutschenreuther, made in Germany, porcelain, 6" long x 1¼" tall. $185.00.

Left: Limoges castle, France, 2½" tall, new. This piece is a deep cobalt blue but shows up black in the picture. Trim is 22K gold. new. $65.00.

Ceramic vases made in China, new, 3½" tall. $10.00 pair.

Porcelain pin tray, 1940s, 3" wide. $25.00.

Bisque toothpick holder, German, 1930s, 3½" long x 1¾" tall. $45.00.

Ceramic, marked England, 1940s, 2" tall. $20.00.

Red clay made by Terra Stone titled "Nicodemus," 3¼" tall. This is very much like Frankoma Pottery. $25.00.

Ceramic, 1950s, 2½" tall x 3" wide. $15.00.

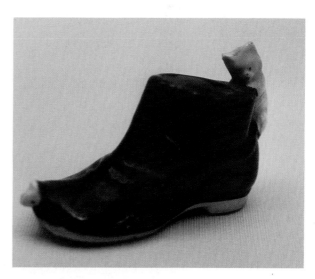

Bone china, marked Lipper & Mann, 1950s. Mama, 2" tall; kittens, 1¼". $20.00 set.

Stone bisque, 1940s, 1¾" tall x 2¼" long. $15.00.

Paper

Advertising card. $3.00 as is.

Advertising card. $5.00.

Salesman's sample of a wooden cigar box label, 8" x 6". $35.00.

Advertising card. $5.00.

Advertising card. $5.00.

Calling card. $5.00.

Advertising card. $3.00 as is.

Advertising card. $5.00.

Autograph book from 1882, 3" x 2". $30.00.

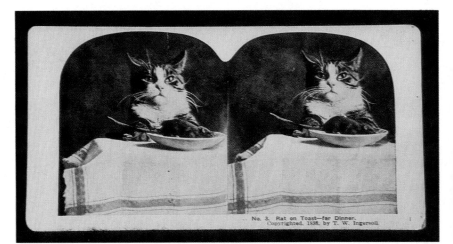

Stereoscopic card. $15.00.

Stereoscopic card. $15.00.

The following four items are Rochester Museum reproductions of early Christmas ornaments, 1986, average size 4". $20.00 set.

Christmas card, 1932. $10.00.

English gift tag, 1987. $5.00.

Papier maché ornament. $10.00.

Left and Right: Kitty Cucumber Christmas cards, 1988, 7" tall. $8.00 – 10.00 each.

Playing cards from 1940. Real cats dressed in clothes. Cards are linen. $20.00.

Playing cards from 1950s. $10.00.

Chesapeake & Ohio Railroad playing cards in plastic case. $65.00.

Chesapeake & Ohio Railroad playing cards. $45.00.

Playing cards from 1940s. $25.00.

First Day Cover, 1988. $10.00.

First Day Cover, 1988. $10.00.

First Day Cover, 1988. $10.00.

The following three items are Kitty Cucumber Christmas present tags, 1988. $15.00 set.

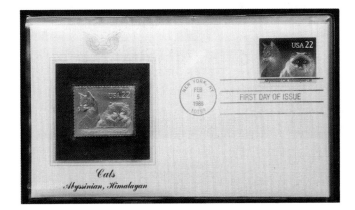

First Day Covers, 1988. $10.00.

Plates and Plaques

German, artist signed not legible, 8¼". $55.00.

New, no maker's name, 8¼". $25.00.

W S George Victorian Cat Capers "Who Is The Fairest Of Them All," 8". $35.00.

Hamilton Country Kittens Collection "Mischief Makers," 8½". $35.00.

Hamilton Collection "Table Manners," 8½". $35.00.

The following four pictures are a set of Staffordshire
England plates, 10½". $100.00 set.

Franklin Mint Christmas plate, 1993 and 1994, 8". $30.00.

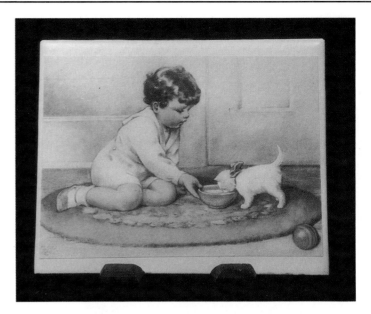

Plaque made in Spain, 1930, 6 x 4¾". $25.00.

Pair of new plaques, 4½" x 4½". $15.00.

Plaque loosely translated "In this house even the cat is nervous," 4" x 5". $20.00.

Postcards

The condition of the postcard determines the price. A mint card has no creases, corners are perfect, and the color is mint. Prices given are for mint cards even though some of them are not. The first 29 cards are actual photographs made into cards. They were mostly printed between 1901 and 1907. Cards signed by the artist command better prices.

$3.00.

$3.00.

$3.00.

$3.00.

$3.00.

$3.00.

$3.00.

$3.00.

$3.00.

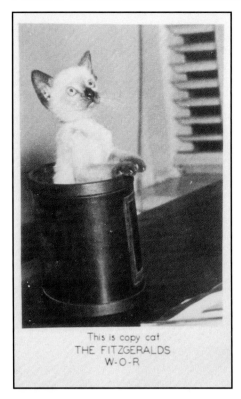

$3.00.

$3.00.

$2.00.

$4.00.

$4.00.

$4.00.

$4.00.

$4.00.

$4.00.

$2.00.

$2.00.

$2.00.

$2.00.

$2.00.

$2.00.

HOT STUFF

$2.00.

$2.00.

$2.00.

$2.00.

$2.00.

$2.00.

$3.00.

$3.00.

$3.00.

$3.00.

$3.00.

$3.00.

$4.00.

$4.00.

$4.00.

$4.00.

$4.00. $4.00.

$4.00. $4.00. $5.00.

$5.00.

Sultan

$4.00.

Mitzi

$4.00. $2.00.

WILL YOU KINDLY PLACE THIS CARD WHERE IT CAN
BE SEEN BY MANY PERSONS?
PRICE, ONE CENT EACH

The Beggar Cat

Poor little beggar cat, hollow-eyed and gaunt,
Creeping down the alley-way like a ghost of want,
Kicked and beat by thoughtless boys, bent on cruel
  play,
What a sorry life you lead, whether night or day!

Hunting after crusts and crumbs, gnawing meat-
  less bones,
Trembling at a human step, fearing bricks and
  stones,
Shrinking at an outstretched hand, knowing only
  blows,
Wretched little beggar cat, born to suffer woes.

Stealing to an open door, craving food and meat,
Frightened off with angry cries and broomed into
  the street.
Tortured, teased, and chased by dog through the
  lonely night,
Homeless little beggar cat, sorry is your plight.

Sleeping anywhere you can, in the rain or snow,
Waking in the cold, gray dawn, wondering where
  to go,
Dying in the street at last, starved to death at that,
Picked up by the scavenger—poor tramp cat!

ELLA WHEELER WILCOX

AMERICAN HUMANE EDUCATION SOCIETY
MASS. S. P. C. A.
180 LONGWOOD AVE., BOSTON, MASS.

$5.00. I defy anyone reading this to end up with dry eyes.

$2.00.

$2.00.

$2.00.

$2.00.

$2.00.

$2.00.

$2.00.

$2.00.

$2.00.

$2.00.

$2.00.

$2.00.

$2.00.

MAY GOOD LUCK GO WITH YOU!

$2.00.

All bound up in this place
Can't leave at present

$2.00.

"ANY USE BEING ON YOUR ROOF 9 O'CLOCK?"

$3.00.

NOBODY EVER. ROCKS ME TO SLEEP.

$2.00.

VERY PROUD

$2.00.

CONTENTED

$2.00.

"Parting is such sweet sorrow."

$3.00.

I'm steering straight for Home, Sweet, Home.

$3.00.

$3.00.

My hair is shaved, my coat is gone,
For sanitary reasons I am told,
What can a poor thing do alone,
Now don't you laugh, for I am cold.

© 1911, V Colby.

$2.00. $2.00.

$2.00.

$2.00.

$2.00.

$3.00.

$3.00.

$3.00.

$3.00.

$3.00.

$3.00.

$3.00.

$3.00.

$3.00.

$3.00.

$3.00.

$3.00.

$4.00.

$4.00.

$4.00.

$4.00.

$4.00.

$5.00.

$5.00.

$5.00.

$3.00.

Pictures and Prints

Watercolor and crayon titled "April's Kittens," 1940s, 18" x 15¼". This is an original made for the cover of the book titled *April's Kittens*. $95.00 – 100.00.

Print, not signed, "Nobody's Purrfect," 20½" x 16½". $35.00.

Print, signed Andrews, "Twin Kittens," 17" x 13½", 1940s. $45.00 – 50.00.

Kitchen print, new, 17" long x 9" wide. $20.00.

Print made in Montclaire, New Jersey, 1903 by artist Arthur M. Morse, 13" x 10". $40.00.

Reverse painting on glass, body of cat is a curly floss, 1940s, 9" x 7". $35.00.

Photogravure published by W.H. Gallgher, New York, NY, in 1906. These engravings are hand colored with watercolors. Artist K.M. MacLean. 13½" x 10½". $300.00 set.

Cheapeake & Ohio Railroad "Chessie"
prints, "Peake Chessies Old Man," 11½"
x 12". $45.00.

Cheapeake & Ohio Railroad "Chessie" prints,
"Chessie and Kittens," 11½" x 12". $45.00.

Cheapeake & Ohio Railroad "Chessie" prints,
"Chessie," 11½" x 12". $45.00.

Black and white photograph enhanced by watercolors signed but not legible, 8" x 10". $35.00.

Silhouette, 4¾" x 3¾", new. $25.00.

Engraving titled "The Vision" by artist Max Standley. 1988, #2 of 50, 12¼" x 12". Wish we could have gotten a closer picture as there is an elf, a snail, and other creatures in the grass. Very fine. $125.00.

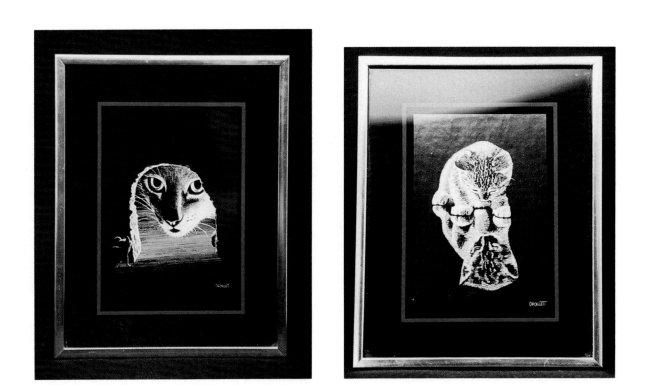

Prints, signed Dorsett, 8" x 10", 1992. $40.00 pair.

Set of prints, 7" x 5¾", signed but not legible, 1940s. $45.00 set.

Puff pictures, signed D. Merlin, 1940s, 6½" x
4½". $20.00 each.

Pastel chalk, no signature, not sure of the age, 10" x 11¼". $55.00.

Print, 1930s, not signed, 10½" x 9½". $45.00.

Puss and Boots cat food giveaway "Dinner Bell," 11" x 8¾", 1940s. $35.00.

Companion piece to the photo on the left, "Special Delivery," 11" x 8¾", 1940s. $35.00.

Print, not signed, 6" x 5", 1940s. $35.00.

Print, not signed, 13" x 10", 1950s. $40.00.

Print, signed Florence Kroger, 1920s, 10½" x 8½". $45.00.

Print, signed Rojanksky, titled "Pussycat Pussycat," 15" x 19". $65.00.

Watercolor, signed Hector, 1990s,
16" x 16". $65.00 – 75.00.

Pastel, signed Rainer, not sure of age, 14" x 16". $125.00.

Print, not signed, 15" x 11¾". $45.00.

Engraving, signed Meta Cluckibaum, titled "Brother
& Sister," 16" x 13", 1940s. $65.00.

Chromo, 15½" x 13", 1920.
$125.00 – 135.00.

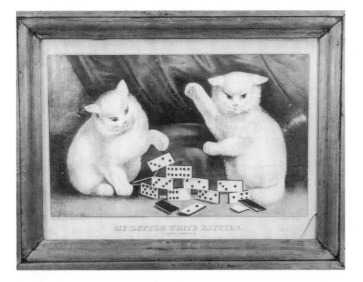

Currier & Ives small folio titled "My Little White Kittens Playing Dominos." $125.00.

Print, signed Clara Turley Newburg, 1948, 11" x 14". $75.00.

Composite of pen & ink drawings, Joan Adams Wickham Originals, 1979, St. Augistine, Florida. Each picture is 3¾" x 3". $85.00 – 95.00.

Print titled "Curiosity," 1940s, 10½" x 10". $45.00.

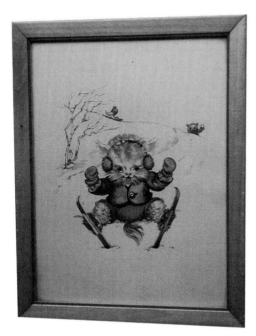

Print, not signed, 8" x 10", 1940s. $35.00.

Foil picture, new, 11" x 12". $25.00.

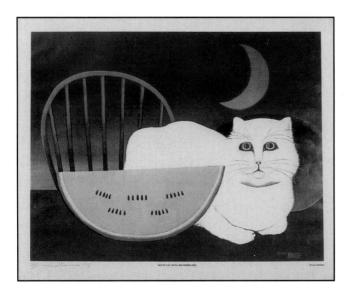

Print by Bruce Wallace, 1978, titled "White Cat With Watermelon," copyright Turtle Bay Gallery, 21" x 17". $50.00.

Print by Bruce Wallace, 1978, titled "Cat With Yarn," copyright Turtle Bay Gallery, 21" x 17". $50.00.

Print, signed G. Vanden Eyckey, 1900, 19¾" x
16¼". $75.00 – 85.00.

Print by Da Wei Kwo from the Kwo Art Studio, titled "TIP," 20" x 15," 1958. $65.00.

Print by Da Wei Kwo from the Kwo
Art Studio, titled "TESS," 20" x 15,"
1958. $65.00.

Steiffs

Steiff animals were made in Germany and are still being made today. The older ones have a metal button in their ear that identifies them as Steiff. Later they had paper labels as they do today. The following Steiffs are from the collection of Robin Tweedie. All information was provided by her.

Kalac, 14", raised button black mohair with white draylon inner ears and pads, bright orange plastic cat eyes, rare, 1950, 14". $500.00 – 600.00.

Kersa, 6½", Puss N Boots, 1940. $200.00.

Tom Cat. Top: 8½". $100.00. Bottom row: A. 4". $150.00. B. 5½". $75.00.

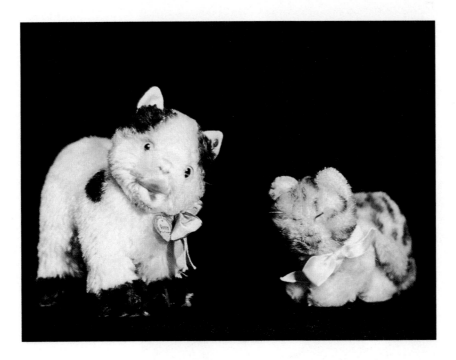

A. Gussy, 6", 1950. $100.00. B. Snurry, 6", 1950. $175.00.

Top row: A. Lizzy, mohair, 8½", 1950. $150.00. B. Cosy Siam, draylon, 8", 1950. $80.00. Bottom row: A. Cattie, draylon, 8½", 1950. $70.00. B. Cattie, draylon, 7", 1950. $65.00.

Top row: A. Siamese, 6", 1950. $80.00. B. Tapsy, 6", 1950. $150.00. C. Gussy, 4", 1950. $120.00. Bottom row: A. Tabby, 7", 1950. $150.00. B. Fiffy, 7", 1950. $150.00.

Top row: A. Lizzy, 7", 1950. $65.00. B. Lizzy, 8½", 1950. $125.00. C. Sitting Cat, 8", 1950. $150.00. Bottom row: A. Sulla, 6½", 1950. $75.00. B. Siamese, 4". $175.00. C. Tabby, 3½", 1950. $45.00.

Top row: A. Floppy Kitty, 6", 1950. $75.00. B. Floppy Kitty, 13", 1950. $125.00. Bottom row: A. Susi, 5", 1950. $120.00. B. Susi, 4", 1950. $90.00. C. Susi, 7", 1950. $175.00.

Top: Fiffy, 10", 1950. $135.00. Bottom: Fiffy, 7", 1950. $75.00.

Top: Kitty, fully jointed, 9½", 1950. $275.00. Bottom: A. Tabby, 6½", 1950. $200.00. B. Tabby, 4", 1950. $150.00.

Schuco yes/no dressed boy and girl kittens, 8½", 1950. $1,000.00 – 1,200.00 for pair.

Humanized cat, draylon, 13", 1960. $100.00.

Lion Cub, 19" long, 1957. This is from Lorraine Greenwood's collection. $275.00.

DIVA, gray, 13¾", 1960. $200.00.

DIVA, white, 13¾", 1960. $200.00.

No name, white, 13", 1960. $200.00.

Miscellaneous

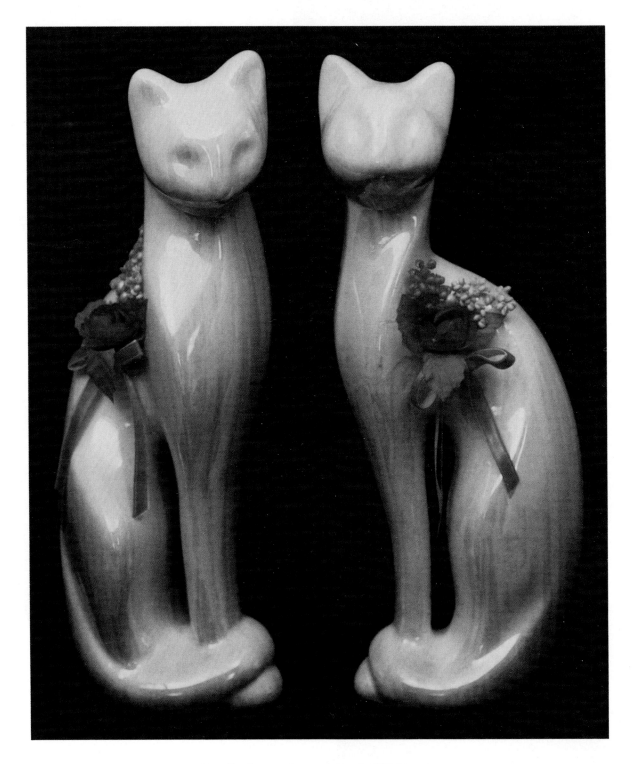

Pearlized ceramic, new, 8" tall. $20.00 pair.

Mohair and excelsior stuffed cat made in Pennsylvania in the 1940s. Has glass eyes. 7" wide x 6¼" tall. $35.00 ea.

Planter from the 1950s, 6½". $15.00.

Kliban cat candy jar, 10" tall. $50.00.

Glass and brass jewelry box, new, 4¼" x 2". $40.00.

Picture frame, 4" x 3", new. $10.00.

Bisque, Capo-di-monti, Enesco Imports, 5½" x 5". $20.00.

Lefton China creamware, 1940s, 5½" long. $20.00.

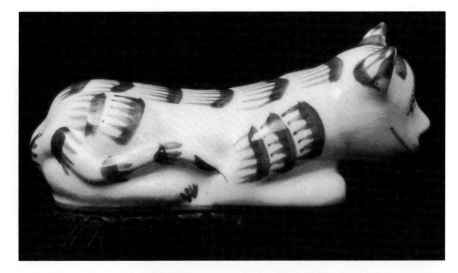

Plaster statue, 1920s, signed but not legible, 18½" tall. $95.00 – 125.00.

Chinese headrest reproduction, 11" long x 6" tall. $45.00.

Lusterware, 1950s, 7" x 6¼". $20.00.

German child's tea set, 1920s. Teapot, 5¼"; creamer, 3¼"; sugar, 2¾"; cup, 2⅛"; plate, 5¼"; saucer, 4¼". $400.00 set.

Bisque cat in hammock, new, 8" wide x 6¼" tall. $15.00.

1950s whimsical cat, 4" tall. $10.00.

Enameled porcelain, new, made in China, 12" tall. $20.00 pair.

Decanter made in Germany, 7" tall. $40.00.

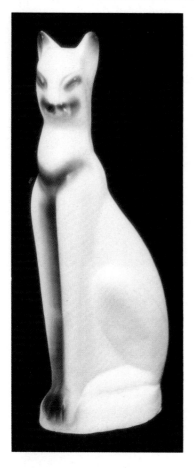

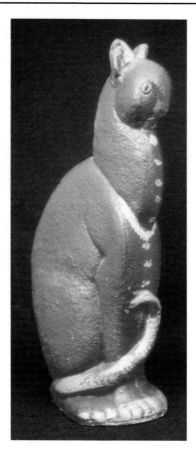

Plaster statue, early 1900s, 12"
tall. $65.00.

Chalkware carnival prize,
1940s, 12½" tall. $50.00.

Chalkware carnival prize bank,
12" tall, 1940s. $65.00 – 70.00.

Royal Haeger ceramic
cat, one glass eye
open and one closed,
1950s, 15¼" tall.
$60.00 – 65.00.

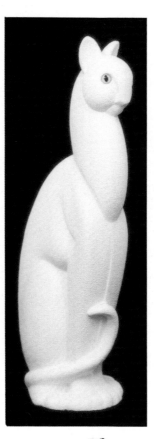

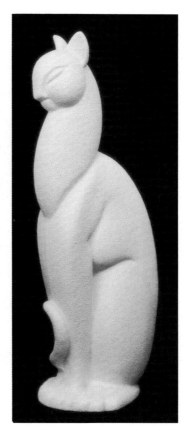

Ceramic, 11" tall, made in Japan, 1940s. $25.00.

Porcelain, 11½" tall, 1940s or earlier, could be English, no mark. $25.00.

Ceramic, 1950s, made in Japan, 11" tall. $15.00.

Royal Copley planter, 1950s, 6½" tall. $25.00.

Ceramic with padded material tail and bow, 1940s. Navy blue: 6¼" tall x 5" long. Red: 4¾" tall x 3¾" long. $35.00 pair.

New pencil holder, made in China, 6¾" tall. $10.00.

Royal Tara bone china "Pet Cat," new, still available through Cash's, Ireland, 6" tall. $25.00.

Airwick giveaway, 1940s, 4" x 8½". $25.00.

Cotton dispenser, new, 5" x 3½". $10.00.

Porcelain, no mark, new, 8¾" tall. $15.00.

Creations by Carol, made in Sevierville, TN, 1983, bonded oak, glass eyes, 4" tall. $35.00.

Made of china, titled "Himalayan," glass eyes, 1956, 7" long x 6" tall. $35.00.

Bone china made in England, 5" tall. Very well made. $25.00 – 30.00.

Ceramic ashtray, probably Italian, 1950s, 6" wide x 5" tall. $20.00.

Made of china, "Black Persian," glass eyes, 1956, 7" x 6". $35.00.

Chalkware, not sure just when it was made. $25.00.

Music box, cats go up and down to the music, 6" tall, new. $15.00.

Music box from the House of Lloyd. New phonograph turns inside globe. If you shake it sparkles fall like snow. $60.00.

Occupied Japan fish bowl hanger made of bisque, 4½" $35.00.

Ceramic cuff bracelets. The left bracelet is the prototype for the right bracelet. Marked K M in a heart, Maui, Hawaii. You would have to have a tiny wrist to wear them. My 10-year-old granddaughter was our model and she is small. $25.00 – 35.00.

Halloween mask, 6" wide, 1960s. $10.00.

Bone china fish bowl hanger, 7" long. $10.00.

Battery operated toy called "Shadow," new, 8" tall. $15.00.

Handmade ceramic tiger, signed GT, 4½" long. This piece is very heavy, stripes deeply incised. I don't know when it was made. $20.00 – 25.00.

Ceramic, made by George Good, Japan, 3½" tall. $10.00.

Battery operated toy, 1960, 8" wide x 9" tall. $25.00.

Redware pottery, new, 4¼" tall. $10.00.

Part of the "Endangered Younguns" series, 1984, 3¾" tall. $15.00.

German, child's cup, 2½" tall. $25.00.

Strange looking bisque cat, new, made in China, 4" tall. $5.00.

German, child's plate, 4" wide. $25.00.

Pair of heavy ceramic cats made in Japan before World War II. Laying cat 6" long. Seated cat 5¼" tall. $35.00 – 40.00 pair.

Tobin Froley Willets Designs limited edition Carousal Cats, bisque, 7" tall. $55.00 – 60.00.

Tobin Froley Willets Designs limited edition Carousal Cats, bisque, 7" tall. $55.00 – 60.00.

Cat with nine lives, 1950s. Big cat, 3¼" tall; small, ¾". $20.00.

Llardro, 4" tall. $55.00 – 65.00.

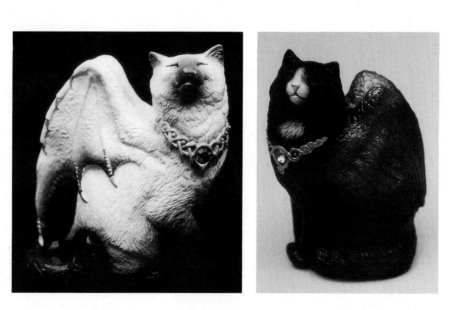

Russian, marked USSR, 3¾" tall. $50.00 – 65.00.

Flap Cats by Windstone, new, limited editions 3¼" tall. $35.00 each.

Royal Haeger planter, 1960s, 8" tall. $35.00.

Bisque, new, made in China, 8" tall. $15.00.

Bisque, made in China, new, 6" tall. $10.00.

Porcelain, 1940s, brass bell and eyelashes, 5" and 4" tall. $15.00 set.

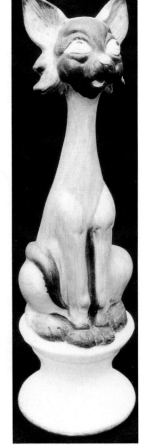

Bisque, made in Japan, new, 5¾". $10.00.

Set of porcelain cats from the 1950s. Mother, 5" tall; babies, 3" tall. $20.00 set.

Ceramic letter holder, 1950s, 6" tall. $20.00.

Pair of porcelain cats, new, 5¼" and 4¾" tall. $10.00 pair.

Chalkware carnival prize bank, 1940s, 6½" tall. $50.00.

Makeup mirror, new, 3¼". $5.00.

Stone Critter, made of resin, 4" long x 3" tall. $25.00.

Bisque cat, 8" long, new. The cat came with the basket. $20.00.

Ceramic leopard, 1940s, 6" long x 3" tall. $10.00.

Bisque, new, made in Japan, 7" long x 5½" tall. $10.00.

Bisque, new, made in Japan, 7" tall x 5" wide. $10.00.

Ceramic, dated 1945, company name is not legible, 7" tall. $20.00.

Sand cast, glass eyes, titled Red Tabby, 5" tall. $25.00.

Celluloid basket with real fur kittens that have glass eyes, 1930s, 5" x 5". $25.00.

Bank, head locks to body with a brass lock, 1940s, 8" tall. $40.00.

Chalkware, 1930s, 5" tall. I have been told that it was part of a set of bookends, the other one had a dog in the chair. $35.00.

Pin dish made by Seymore Mann, 1992, 5" tall. $20.00.

Ceramic piece from Italy, 1950s. Each piece was put on by hand. There is damage to the piece but it is still very nice. $85.00 if perfect. $40.00 as is.

Flower vase, 1970s, 3¾" tall. $15.00.

Handmade ceramic, dated 1975, Holland Mold Co., 5" tall x 4" wide. $10.00.

A pretty new kitty, 6"; tall, satin ribbon roses. $10.00.

Bisque, new, no marks, 10" long. $15.00.

Pin dish, 1950s, 4" tall. $10.00.

Ceramic, marked made in England, probably 1970s, 6½" long. $45.00.

Lefton China, made in the 1950s, 6¼" tall x 5" wide. $25.00.

Very stylized cat made of red clay. I have been told it came from Virginia and was made in 1980, 7" long x 6" tall. $25.00.

Ceramic made by Seymore Mann, new, 8½" long x 4" tall. $35.00.

Bisque, new, 5¼" wide x 4" tall. $15.00.

Royal Copley planter, 1940s, 3¾" tall. $20.00.

Harvey Knox Kingdom made by Global Art, 4¼" tall x 3" wide. $25.00.

Bisque, new. Laying, 4½" long; seated, 3" x 3". $10.00 pair.

Pair of new bisque dolls, 9" tall. $15.00 pair.

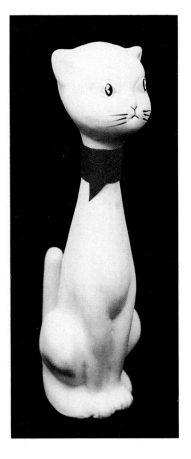

Bubble bath bottle made of rubber with cork in the bottom, 1950s, 10" tall. $30.00.

Molded resin made by Enesco, new, 2¾" tall. $15.00.

Ceramic made in the 1940s, marked N in a circle, 5" x 5". $25.00.

Ceramic, 1950s, velvet bow ties, 7" x 6¼" tall. $15.00 pair.

Bone china, 1960s, 7½" and 7¼" tall. $20.00 pair.

Ceramic, 1950s, 6½" tall. $10.00.

Ceramic made by Bestwick in England, 5½" long x 4" tall. $65.00.

Ceramic, 1950s 13" tall. Very well made. $30.00 pair.

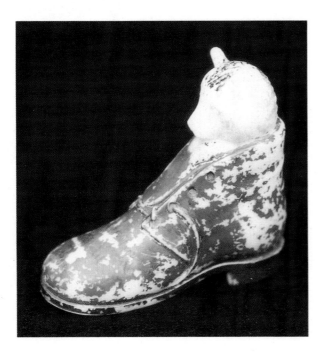

Old milk glass shoe, original paint, 1920s, made in Pennsylvania, 3" tall x 4" wide. $55.00.

Porcelain made in Germany, shield mark, 1930s, 4½" tall x 4" wide. $35.00 – 45.00.

Porcelain, 1950s, no mark, 10" long x 5" tall. $25.00 – 30.00.

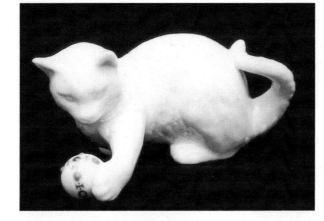

Lenox, new, 5" long, $65.00 – 75.00.

Lenox, new, 5" tall. $65.00 – 75.00.

Lenox, new, 5" long x 2¾" tall. $65.00 – 75.00.

Lenox, new, 4" long. $65.00 – 75.00.

Bisque condiment set made in Japan. I have seen this marked Occupied Japan. Mustard, 5½" tall; shakers, 3" tall. $75.00.

Porcelain made by Bestwick in England, 8" tall, 1960s. $65.00.

Marked made by Anna Lee, 1990, 10" tall x 8½" long. This is one of the cutest pieces we shot. $25.00.

"Lucifer," part of the Disney Collection, 4" long x 3¼" tall. $125.00.

Bisque, 1950s, titled "Silver Persian," 7¼" x 5¼" tall. $35.00.

Planter, 1960s, 6" tall. $15.00.

The First Cat "Socks," new, 10" long x 6¼" tall. $25.00.

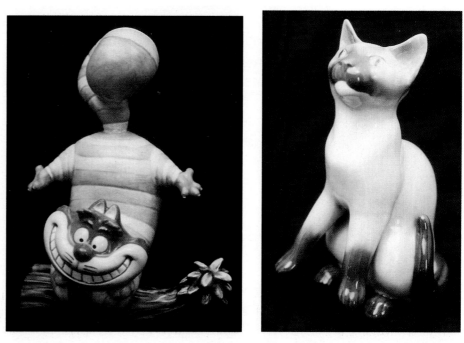

Planter, 1940s, 6" tall. $15.00.

"Cheshire Cat," Disney Collection, 5" tall. This was only available to members. $135.00.

Bing & Grundahl, new, 5¼". $135.00.

Plastic yarn holder, 1940s, 5" x 5". $25.00.

Doorstop, new, plaster, 10½" tall x 8" wide. $15.00.

Max Factor "MYSTIC" perfume, probably 1960s, 5½" tall. $25.00.

Royal Copley planter, 1950s, 5¼" tall x 4" wide. $25.00.

Ceramic, marked TISO, 1950s, 7½" tall. $20.00.

Ceramic, 1950s, 6¼" tall. $15.00.

Note paper holder, new, 7" tall. $8.00 – 10.00.

Early mohair, circa 1920, maker unknown, 8" tall. Robin Tweedie collection. $200.00.

Pencil holder, marked Tanckashai, San Francisco, 1990, 6" tall. $10.00.

Mohair kittens on a pillow, maker unknown, 1960s. Robin Tweedie Collection. $50.00.

Porcelain, 1920s, 5½" long, no marks. $35.00 – 40.00.

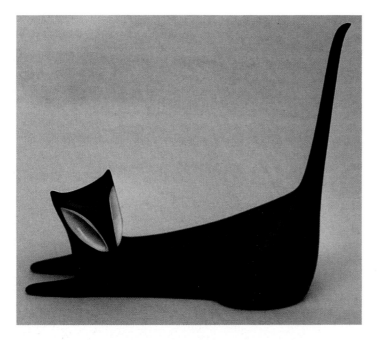

Royal Dux, 1950s, 7" long x 7" tall. $150.00.

Staffordshire ring box, lid marked with impressed shield and numbers, early 1900s, 5" tall. $150.00 – 175.00.

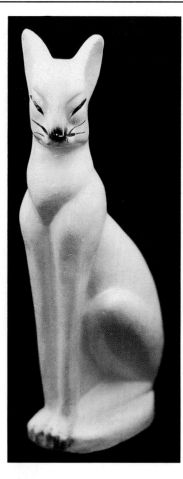

Bisque cat seated on silk pillow, 1930s, 4" tall x 2" wide. Chair is some sort of molded material. $35.00 – 45.00.

Goebel, Germany, 4" tall. $35.00.

Chalkware carnival prize, 1940s, 14½" tall. $50.00.

Plastic jewelry box, 1940s, 6¼" wide x 4" tall. $25.00.

Tidy-cat giveaway. $7.00 – 10.00.

Ceramic pin dish, new, 3¼" tall. $10.00.

Satsuma-type ring dish, 4½" tall, new. $20.00.

Avon bottle. $10.00.

Avon bottle. $10.00.

Goebel, Germany, 3" tall. $20.00.

Stuffed kittens in musical basket, new, 7¼" tall x 7" long. They move to the music. $15.00.

Bone china, 1970s, 3" tall. $10.00.

Lefton China, porcelain, real whiskers, 3" tall. $15.00.

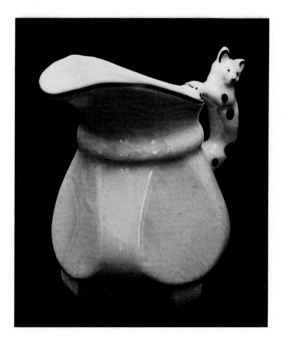

Czechoslovakian luster pitcher, 1940s, 4½" tall. $25.00.

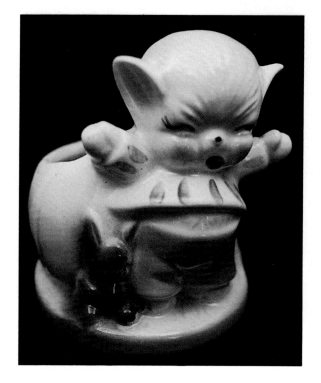

Royal Copley planter, 1950s, 5" tall. $25.00.

Elizabeth Arden ring dish, came with perfume, 6" long. $20.00.

Ceramic bank, think this is new, 6" tall x 5" wide. $20.00.

Cumbria made in England for QVC, 5" tall, molded resin. $45.00 – 50.00.

Cumbria made in England for QVC, 5¾" tall, molded resin. $45.00 – 50.00.

Papier maché bank, new, marked Royal Designs, 4½" tall. $30.00.

Red clay ceramic, impressed with a deer mark, each 3" tall. $35.00 set.

Pair of chalkware cats, 5" tall and 3" tall. $20.00 set.

Creamware, 1940s, 4" tall. $15.00.

Creamware planter, 1940s, 5" tall. $10.00.

Ceramic bank, new, 6" tall. $15.00.

Ceramic planter, new, 6" tall. $10.00.

Set of new porcelain cats. Seated, 6" tall; laying, 6" long x 4½" tall. $25.00 set.

Molded resin shoe, new, 3¼" tall. $10.00.

Ceramic shoe, 1940s, 6" long. $15.00.

Porcelain shoe flower vase, 1940s, 4" tall. $10.00 – 15.00.

Porcelain, made in Japan, 1950s, 4¼" tall. $10.00.

Stone Critter, glass eyes, new, 4" tall. $20.00.

Royal Doulton, England, 4" tall. $55.00.

Pair of new porcelain cats made for QVC, 6" tall. $25.00 pair.

Bisque, new, QVC, 8" long. $25.00.

Porcelain, impressed mark Germany 7899 Erphilia. This cat was pictured in my first book as unknown (plate 318). $50.00.

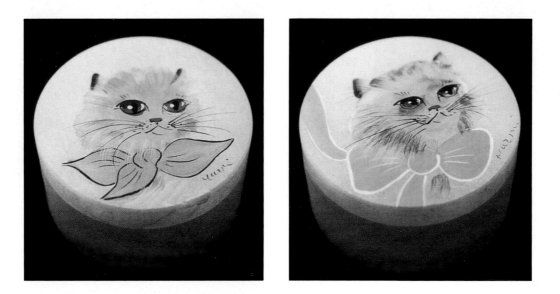

Alabaster boxes made for QVC, 3" wide x 1½" tall. $15.00 ea.

Royal Doulton, new, 4½" long x 3" tall. $35.00 – 40.00.

Ceramic, made in Mexico, 5" tall x 3" wide. $8.00 – 10.00.

Cloisonne made for the Winterhut Collection, 5" long x 3" tall. $85.00.

Porcelain, very heavy, new, 5" tall x 6½" wide. $20.00.

Porcelain, very heavy, new, 6" tall x 5" wide. $20.00.

Ceramic, 1950s, made in Japan, 5½" tall. $15.00.

Ceramic, marked Coventry USA, 1950s, 5" tall. $15.00.

Ceramic, possibly made in Portugal or Spain, new, 7" tall. $20.00.

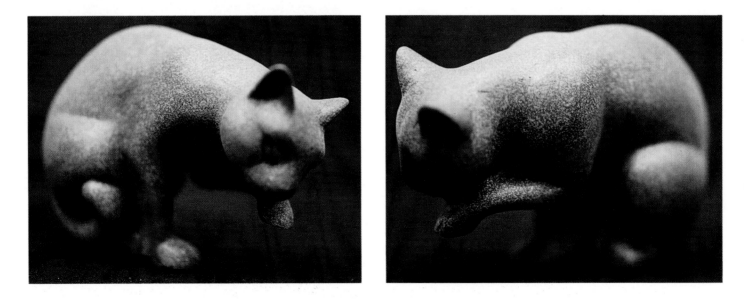

Franklin Mint bronze, "Message Of Happiness" by Yao Yoo-Xin, 5½" long x 4" tall. $150.00.

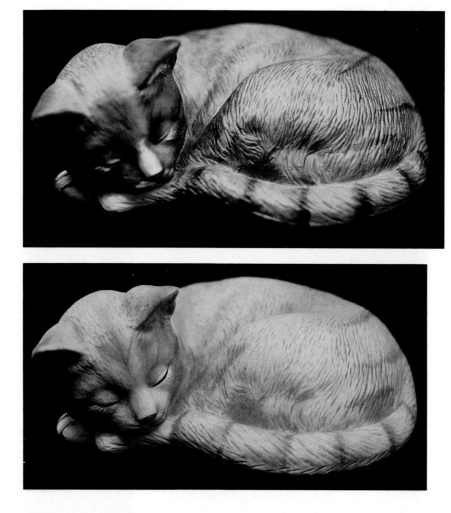

Bisque by Ebeling Ross, new, 7" long. $20.00 each.

Bisque Seymore Mann music box, 3" long x 5½" tall, new. $30.00.

Molded resin, new, 3" tall x 4" wide. $15.00.

The following 6 photos are Dipinto & Mano, Italy, made of bisque for QVC. Laying, 5" long; half seated, 4" tall; full seated, 5¼" tall. $30.00 each set.

Lefton creamware, 1950s, 4" tall. $20.00.

Royal Doulton, new, 4" tall. $35.00.

Seymore Mann music box, 5" long x 3" tall, new. $25.00.

Porcelain, 1940s, no mark, well made, 4¾" tall. $20.00 pair.

Chinese embroidery on silk, new, 9" tall x 5" wide. Cat is the same on both sides in rosewood frame. $15.00 – 20.00.

Molded resin on satin pillow, new, 5" long. $12.00 – 15.00.

Cortendorf, made in West Germany, 1964, 12½" tall. $65.00 – 75.00.

Elizabeth King Brown Designs musical, turns to music, 4½" long. $20.00.

Bisque, 4" long in 5¼" long basket, new. $15.00.

Red clay pottery, made in Hot Springs, GA, 1970s, 3" tall. $20.00 – 25.00.

Made in Portugal, 1950s. Large cat, 12" long x 7½" tall; small, 6" long x 4" tall. $35.00 pair.

Musical covered dish made by Coby "Cat Duet," 4" long x 1½" tall. $45.00 – 50.00.

Coby "Kitten & Canary," 4" long x 1½" tall. $45.00 – 50.00.

Coby "Alley Cat," 4" long x 1½" tall. $45.00 – 50.00.

Coby "Kitten on the Keys," 3" wide x 1½" tall. $45.00 – 50.00.

Coby "Owl & the Pussycat," 3½" wide x 1½" tall. $45.00 – 50.00.

Porcelain cat in the manner of Llardro, 3" tall. $20.00.

Reproduction Satsuma, made in China, 4" long. $10.00.

Bisque, made in Japan, new, 7" long. $15.00.

Paperweight, 1920s, 3" x 2¼". $55.00.

Hutschenreuther, made in Germany, 4" long x 3" tall. $165.00.

Llardro, 5¾" long. $90.00 – 95.00.

Piano baby, made in Germany, 1920s, 6" long. $100.00 – 125.00.

Porcelain, W.R. Midwinter Ltd., Burslem, England, 6¼". $45.00 – 50.00.

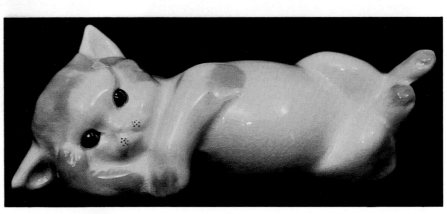

Czechoslovakian child's feeding dish, 1930s, 3¾" wide. $65.00.

Bavarian luster child's dish, 1920s, 6¾" wide. $50.00.

Child's dish, possibly German, 3¾" wide, 1930s. $65.00.

Child's dish, no marks, 1930s, 6¾" wide. $65.00.

Left and above: Bisque Christmas ornaments, new, 2½" tall. $25.00 set of six.

Pair of bisque cats made in China, new, 4" tall. $10.00 pair.

Hutschenreuther, made in Germany, 7¾" tall x 6¼" wide. $400.00.

Porcelain, Erphilia, Germany, 8½" long. $65.00 – 75.00.

Pitcher, made in Germany, 4" tall, 1910. $125.00.

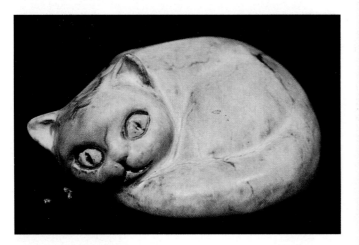

Ceramic, new, 5" long. $15.00.

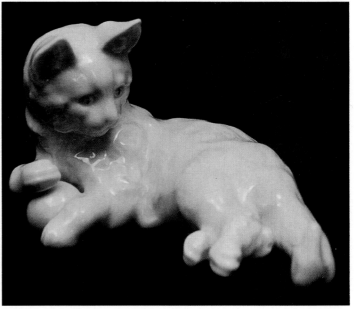

Hutchenreuther, made in Germany, 5¼" wide x 2¼" tall. $165.00.

Porcelain, no mark, 1950s, 6¼" long. $35.00.

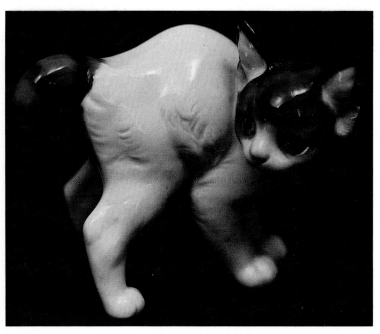

Rosenthal, 4¾" wide x 3¼" tall. $165.00.

Ceramic cats covered with material and glazed, 10" tall and 8" tall. $25.00 pair.

Czechoslovakian luster pitcher, 1930s, 5" tall. $45.00 – 50.00.

Llardro, 7½" tall. This was in the first book (plate 452) and was not identified as Llardro. $65.00.

Made in Spain, new, 4" tall x 3" wide. $20.00.

Museum reproduction of a Chinese piece, 1970s, 4¾" tall. $25.00.

Stone Critter, new, 3¾" tall. $25.00.

Red clay pottery, made in China, new. Seated, 4" tall; standing, 3" tall. $15.00 pair.

Rosenthal, 5" tall. $150.00 – 165.00.

Stone Critter, new, glass eyes, 4" tall. This is the perfect image of my fat cat named "Misty." $25.00.

Hand-painted chalkware, not sure how old, but very well done, 7" tall. $35.00.

Danbury Mint Christmas ornaments. This is the balance of collection shown in the first book. $20.00 ea.

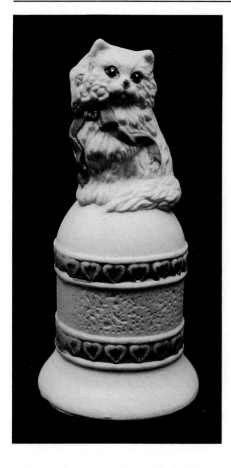

Ceramic bell, new, 4½" tall. $5.00.

Ceramic bell, new, 3¾" tall. $10.00.

Bisque bell, new, 5¼" tall. $10.00.

Bisque bell, new, 2½" tall. $5.00.

Ceramic planter, 1940s 4" tall x 3¼" wide. $20.00.

Ceramic, 1930s, marked Patent Pending, 8½" x 8½". $50.00.

Hutschenreuther, made in Germany, porcelain, 5" tall x 4" wide. $165.00.

Early mohair cat, 1920, maker unknown, 9" tall. Robin Tweedie collection. $200.00.